April Sixth

JOHN C. LEFGREN

FOREWORD BY
TRUMAN G. MADSEN

Deseret Book Company
Salt Lake City, Utah
1980

Library of Congress Cataloging in Publication Data

Lefgren, John C   1945-
    April sixth.

    Includes index.
    1. Jesus Christ—Nativity—Miscellanea.
2. Mormons and Mormonism—Doctrinal and controversial
works.   I. Title.
BX8643.J4L43   232.9'21   80-11199
ISBN 0-87747-810-4

Contents

Acknowledgments

The original inspiration for this book came in Finland one evening in the early spring of 1977 when I was reading the eighth chapter of Third Nephi in the Book of Mormon. Since that evening I have searched for the chronological harmony of April sixth. The book evolved in two parts: first the numbers and then the words. Dr. Dan Pascu from the Nautical Almanac Office of the U.S. Naval Observatory in Washington, D.C., provided invaluable technical assistance and direction in understanding the numbers. After that Mark Reynolds, a good friend, encouraged me to write the book. Then the literary talents of Glenn Clark came into play, and I was able to finish a draft for submission to the publisher. Robert F. Smith of Independence, Missouri, improved the book with a careful and thoroughly professional review of the manuscript. Finally, my thanks go to Truman Madsen for his foreword.

Foreword

by Truman G. Madsen

We live in a world of scientific technology, a period in which much is known of astronomy, the positions of the stars, the interrelations of the solar system. In our lifetime men have planted flags on the moon and taken close-up photographs of Mercury and Jupiter. At the same time, we live in an era of rampant superstition. Astrology, numerology, and occultism flourish. Today more time and money are spent on the pseudocalculations of horoscopes and the like than on parlor games. One of the superstitions of the irreligious is that our personalities, our behavior, our very lives are controlled by sidereal movements.

For those who have ears to hear, modern revelation has reenthroned the truth: the stars and their interrelationships and rotations do not dominate us. But the sun, the moon, and the stars are positioned and controlled by the Creator of "worlds without number," and "any man who hath seen any or the least of these hath seen God moving in his majesty and power." (D&C 88:47.)

Further, we are promised that the time will come when "all the times of their revolutions, all the appointed days, months, and years, and all the days of their days, months, and years, and all their glories, laws, and set times, shall be revealed in the days of the dispensation of the fulness of times." (D&C 121:31.)

And someday we will understand that which was ordained unto us "in the midst of the Council of the Eternal God of all other gods before this world was." (D&C 121:32.)

Thus, though our schedulings and calculations are often inaccurate and inept, there is an order of things. There are laws "irrevocably decreed" (D&C 130:20) and yet by us "voluntarily subscribed to" (*History of the Church* 6:51). Our freedom expands most when it is synchronized with the right time and place—not too early, not too late. The analogy extends to the total extent of our lives and their unfolding. And whether one defines time by the metaphor of an inclined plane, or a recurrent cycle, or as an ever-widening and heightening spiral, there is a close kinship between time and space. The Prophet Joseph Smith writes, following Abraham, of time as calculable in spatial units: "cubits." (See facsimile 2, Pearl of Great Price.)

The order of creation itself leads to a divine mandate rooted in time—a Sabbath. The living influence of that we once saw vividly in the home of a Jewish rabbi on Mt. Carmel. A spirit of celebration shone through his table manner, and we learned that it derived from his father and his father's father. "Tell us about your Sabbath," we said. With light in his eyes he described the pulling of the curtains as the first twilight stars became visible on Friday night; the gathering of his family freshly bathed and dressed and full of expectation; his wife's immaculate preparations—the special silver, the candles, the twisted loaves, the finest of meat and fish. He spoke of offering the memory-drenched traditional prayers on his children, of the passing of bread, the singing of ancient hymns and the morning synagogue service. He explained that it was out of phase with their Sabbath to discuss the raw military crisis outside or to fritter the day away in commercial entertainment. Instead they follow time-honored, elevating moments. They open the Torah and review intimately the epic of Abraham and Moses. Strictness, he acknowledged, permeates Sabbath observance, for laws upon laws upon laws surround the day. The Talmud is full of them. Yet its meaning and rhythm brings newness, refreshment, rejoicing. On this day denial is combined with ennobling pleasure, the closing out of the world of work and the pulling in of the intimate consciousness of the Creator, the partaking anew of his choicest elements and acts. All of this, the rabbi pointed out, had roots in the commandment of God on Mount Sinai. And his people have a saying, "More than the Jews have kept the Sabbath, the Sabbath has kept the Jews."

The celebration of Shabat on each successive seventh day is extended by the Bible and by Jewish tradition from days to years. Thus in Jewish reckoning the seventh year is a sabbatical year, and seven times seven years becomes a jubilee year, a year of release from debt, the lifting of the downtrodden, a time of compassionate relief.

Our modern scriptures elaborate the same pattern in terms of centuries and millennia. We are taught that there are seven one-thousand-year periods in the earth's appointed history following Adam. At the dawn of the seventh of these periods the earth itself will be transformed and will begin its own Sabbath. (D&C 77:12-13.) So, in appropriate order, will the human family.

Among the peoples of Abraham, there are other long-lived traditions about the beginning day of the new year. The Jews believe Moses designated it the first day of Nisan, which in our present calendar would be in early April. Some Jewish traditions (presently unconfirmable) say that this was the day of creation of our universe. On the same day, they say, Adam and Eve partook of the forbidden fruit; it was the day therefore of both their death and new life. Tradition further says it was the birthday of both Abraham and Jacob as well as the day of their death; that it was the day when Sarah, Rachel, and Hannah, all three barren, were visited and promised fruitfulness; and that it was the day Moses parted and crossed the Red Sea.

Also in the spring, observant Jews celebrate the most pervasive and lasting nature festival in Judaism, the Passover. It commemorates the deliverance of Israel from the slavery, idolatry, and darkness of Egypt. Traditionally, the feast of the Passover was a gathering feast. Hordes of people converged on Jerusalem and the temple. Temple priests and Levites prepared offerings known as the atonement offering and the thank offering. Lambs were roasted whole with no bones broken. After the destruction of the temple in 72 A.D., Passover was kept alive in homes. In the Talmud is a saying that at the time of the coming messiah sacrifices will be resumed in the restored temple (and so also says the "Temple Scroll" dated about 150 B.C., discovered twenty years ago near the Dead Sea) as a thank offering, a clear ritual of gratitude. Today the Passover order of Seder is a feast, an indelible visual aid enabling all, from the venerably old to the lisping child, to retell and passionately relive the Exodus story, Israel's emerging from bondage into the wilderness of trial and then into a land of milk and honey. The foods of Passover—the unleavened bread, the bitter herbs, the sacred goblets of wine—merge with the chorus recitations and the songs. All keep the memory green and the promise of "next year in Jerusalem" powerful.

Here again, timing is laden with traditional symbolism. The Bible says that Moses and his people left Egypt by the light of the full moon, the moon of the spring equinox, at midnight on the fourteenth night of Nisan. In both Jewish and Moslem traditions the lunar year is composed of twelve moon-months of twenty-nine or thirty days each. But the solar year that determines the seasons extends an additional eleven days. Thus in merely three years the Passover date would lapse or fall behind by nearly a month. Hence the Jews established a "leap month" and arranged perpetually to adjust their calendar with seven leap months every nineteen years. What this has achieved, over more than two thousand years, is the keeping of the Passover celebration intimately connected to the spring equinox. In lands and climes where there are observant Jews, this timing has been carefully followed. Our day of powerful communication and world-shrinking travel makes it unnecessary to do what the Jews did for centuries: send out from Jerusalem the word that the moon crescent would come on the twenty-ninth or thirtieth day of the month. Even now some Jews, "just to be sure," double up and hold two days of the initial Passover celebration.

Echoes of such sacred commemoration of time and place have been revitalized in the restoration. Thus, for example, one of the meanings of *temple* is that, like a template, it exactly fits a position in relation to the cosmos. Temples are sometimes spoken of as observatories from which and in which we "get our bearings" on life and the universe. A perfect temple is built foursquare by the compass facing east and bounded by perimeters that are exactly south, west, and north.

The Prophet Joseph Smith declared that if the "strict order of the priesthood" were followed, the First Presidency of the Church would lay the southeast corner of the temple and then the others would be laid in succession. (See *History of the Church* 4:331.) Brigham Young explained that the southeast corner of the temple was laid first "because there is the most light," and in Manti he laid the temple cornerstone in the season of spring, the time of increased life and light, at high noon, the day's moment of greatest light.

In the Salt Lake Temple, the designs and intentions of Brigham Young and his architects are similarly symbolic. On the west tower the constellation Ursa Major points to the north or polar star, signifying, as architect Truman O. Angell wrote, the "one true way" of the Master's priesthood. Not as easily recognized is the temporal significance of the carefully chiseled successive crescents of the moon presided over by sunstones. These represent in sequence the lunar phases of the moon. Traced in harmony with our calendar, they make the center of the east tower a testimony in stone to a crucial date: April 6—the day of the temple's dedication (as, forty years earlier, of the laying of its cornerstone), the day of the birth of the restored church "out of obscurity and out of darkness," and the beginning of the new and all-inclusive dispensation when "the morning breaks and the shadows flee."

Orson Pratt, perhaps influenced by the Prophet Joseph Smith's account of celestial time in the Abraham facsimiles, understood the parable of the Lord of the field (D&C 88) to be teaching this: the "joy of the countenance" of the Lord is experienced by world systems and planets in succession, from the last unto the first and from the first unto the last, everyone in his own order until "his hour" is finished. Thus, Elder Pratt concluded, "Each planetary kingdom is visited by its Creator in its time and season." Likewise the "inhabitants of each planet are blessed with the presence and visits of their Creator."

Now, as to what all this prefigures and in retrospect commemorates: This volume presents a collection of evidence, including the self-consistent chronology of the Book of Mormon, that in the spring of the year, precisely on April 6, the glorious Messiah was born, descending into the world as an infant in a grotto in Bethlehem. Thirty-three years later, the resurrected Messiah emerged from the borrowed tomb of Joseph of Arimathea, the firstfruits of them that slept. In the same season, in the midst of Passover, was his sacrifice-offering, his descent in Gethsemane into the agony of all the human family and on Golgotha to his cataclysmic death on the cross. Here are the events and meanings that undergird all other events and meanings. Here is the focus of time and season, of place and event, that measures all else—events that are at the fulcrum of the cosmos and of the living source of our lives. April's amazing meaning is evident through and through the messianic message.

On the eve of Christ's last supper, if he followed the patterns of Jewish rite exactly, there would have come a moment, as there had in every earlier Passover feast for centuries, when the youngest son at the table (it might have been John the Beloved) asked in that upper room, "What is different about tonight?" And in his heart facing the darkest and yet most brilliant night of his life, the Master may have asked and answered the harder question of an earlier faithful son, "Father, where is the sacrifice?"

How many feelings, how many colors of life, how much of eternity was drawn into one day and season in his soul: birth and death, life and higher life, anguish and rejoicing, depths and heights.

When the Redeemer's hour had come, Book of Mormon prophets say the earth itself shuddered and exclaimed, "The God of nature suffers." Just as well it could rejoice, as does our hymn, "Nature breathes her sweetest fragrance on the holy Sabbath day." At his second coming it may well cry out, "The God of transformed nature has touched his glorified foot to the Mount of Olives." And the mountains shall flow down at his presence.

But was it all really in April?

Consider the latest evidence.

CHAPTER 1

April Sixth

"The rise of the Church of Christ in these last days, being one thousand eight hundred and thirty years since the coming of our Lord and Savior Jesus Christ in the flesh, it being regularly organized and established agreeable to the laws of our country, by the will and commandments of God, in the fourth month, and on the sixth day of the month which is called April." (D&C 20:1.)

The Church of Jesus Christ of Latter-day Saints was organized "by the will and commandments of God" on Tuesday, April 6, 1830. That date was chosen by the Lord as the "precise day upon which, according to his will and commandment, we [Joseph Smith and five other men] should proceed to organize his Church once more here upon the earth." (Preface to D&C 20.) The Doctrine and Covenants implies that the birth of Jesus Christ was an important factor in the selection of this precise date.

Those few members who met with the young American prophet, Joseph Smith, in the Peter Whitmer home in Fayette, New York, to organize and establish once more the

Church of Christ accepted April 6, 1830, as the completion of "one thousand eight hundred and thirty years since the coming of our Lord and Savior Jesus Christ in the flesh." (D&C 20:1.) For the last century and a half Latter-day Saints have continued to believe that the timing of the restoration of the Church of Christ has an association with the birth of Christ.[1] Their acceptance of this association is based on their faith in a revelation given through the Prophet Joseph. The significance of April sixth was never presented as the result of chronological research or scriptural interpretation. It was identified "by the spirit of prophecy and revelation." (Preface to D&C 20.)

Modern scripture implies that Jesus Christ was born in the year 1 B.C. In our day most scholars critically dismiss the likelihood of fixing that year as the time of our Lord's birth. Some rationalize that Joseph Smith naively accepted the year of his calendar as representing the length of time since the first coming of Christ. Such an approach discounts the likelihood of finding any meaningful or concrete reference to the timing of Christ's birth in the Doctrine and Covenants. It diminishes any likely association between the birth of Christ and the restoration of the Church of Christ. It pushes the significance of D&C 20:1 into a category that some are prepared to characterize as "Mormon folklore."

I believe that time has meaning to God. I believe he has spoken and will speak through his prophets about the timing of events that have occurred, are occurring, or will occur. I believe that the test of most prophecies includes an element of time. Prophecy often looks forward to particular events as occurring in a particular sequence. Prophecy may also identify the timing of past events.

In one of the great revelations of modern time we read that "all the times of their revolutions, all the appointed days, months, and years, and all the days of their days, months, and years, and all their glories, laws, and set times, shall be revealed in the days of the dispensation of the fulness of times." (D&C 121:31.) I believe that this verse of

2

scripture is not just poetic, but may also be interpreted literally. I accept as a matter of faith that during the current dispensation, which began with Joseph Smith, the times and seasons of the past will come forth.

The scriptures tell us that Jesus Christ came into the dimensions of this earth's time and space during the meridian of time. (See Moses 6:57.) For centuries believers have longed and searched for the time of the Messiah's coming. Many do still. In a way this writing is in that tradition, but instead of looking to the future it looks back through the last two millennia and measures as accurately as possible the flow of time. The approach is simple and direct; some may consider it too narrow. But I believe that the scriptures contain accurate historical narratives whose few but explicit references to historical dates are to be taken seriously. These dates, more than anything else, give to the scriptural record historical dimensions that can be measured and understood.

It seems to me that in the twentieth century one cannot "discover" the day of Christ's birth. It has been available for the last one hundred and fifty years for all to read and believe. It is possible, however, to show, independent of the statement of Joseph Smith, that the night of April 5-6, 1 B.C. (Gregorian calendar), can be identified as the time of the birth of the historic Jesus of Nazareth. In doing this I have used modern calculating facilities. I have consulted those who are charged with measuring and keeping time for the United States and with others who have spent their professional lives studying the calendars of the ancients. I have examined closely the structure and function of first century calendars used among the Jews as well as the reckoning of time in pre-Columbian America.

There are essentially three steps in my research. First, I identify a Friday occurring at the time of Passover that satisfies the New Testament chronology of the crucifixion. The probable hour and day of the crucifixion thus becomes a fixed point in the time by which we currently reckon.

3

Second, I translate the length of Christ's life into a specific number of days as given by a record kept by a people in the western hemisphere during the first century. (These people witnessed both the signs of Christ's birth and those of his death.) Having established the likely day and hour of Christ's death and the length of his life, I am then able to determine the likely time of his birth by reckoning backwards from the hour of his death. This approach produces the night of April 5-6, 1 B.C. (Gregorian calendar), as the time of Christ's birth—a time identified by prophecy and revelation as being associated with the birth of Christ.

My analysis links three historic events: the birth of Christ, the death and resurrection of Christ, and the nineteenth-century restoration of the Church of Christ. All these events are chronologically linked in Table 4 for those who are interested in following the precise calculations. My intention is to present the material in a very direct and straightforward way. Every step of the calculations will be made clear, to those who want to verify the calculations, by careful examination of text and notes. The message I am trying to give, however, is more profound than a mathematical proof. The religious symbolism of the association of the birth of Christ with the restoration of the Church of Christ is worthy of careful contemplation.

The reader may wish to follow this line of approach:

1. Establish in your own mind a clear understanding of how it is possible to determine the likely day of Christ's death from the account in the New Testament and the lunar Passover feast of the Jewish calendars.

2. Determine to your own satisfaction how ancient American calendars function, and then attempt to measure the length of Christ's life as it is given in the Book of Mormon.

3. With Christ's probable death date and the length of his mortal life established, identify a likely time during which Christ was born—which will be found to be the night of April 5-6, 1 B.C. (Gregorian calendar).

4

4. Measure the number of solar years elapsed between the thus-calculated time of Christ's birth to the date of the restoration of the Church—which will be found to be exactly 1,830.

5. Then ask yourself how a young man living in the rural districts of early nineteenth-century America could have calculated those dates and lapse of time, which we only now independently find to be in harmony with ancient calendars, history, and scriptures, and with the fixed movements of the earth, sun, and moon.

CHAPTER 2

Measuring Time

"And again, verily I say unto you, he hath given a law unto all things, by which they move in their times and their seasons; And their courses are fixed, even the courses of the heavens and the earth, which comprehend the earth and all the planets. And they give light to each other in their times and in their seasons, in their minutes, in their hours, in their days, in their weeks, in their months, in their years—all these are one year with God, but not with man. The earth rolls upon her wings, and the sun giveth his light by day, and the moon giveth her light by night, and the stars also give their light, as they roll upon their wings in their glory, in the midst of the power of God." (D&C 88:42-45.)

To any person, the most important measure of the passage of time is in the events of his own life. We all mark off time by major events that occur only once. Time has meaning, indeed, only as the measure of relation of one

6

event to another. For all people, the most important life is the life of Christ, for his life makes it possible for all to have life after death.

The mortal Christ lived in time. His earthly life had a beginning and an end. His birth and death can be reckoned as discrete events in the flow of time we understand, experience, and measure. This book centers on three points in time: the birth of Christ, the death of Christ, and Christ's historic, nineteenth-century restoration of the pristine Christian church of the meridian of time.

Because we can measure time, we can begin to understand it. We are as certain of the existence of any day falling two thousand years ago as we are certain of the existence of the day before yesterday. There may be some uncertainty as to the events that occurred on a given day in history—uncertainty stemming only from a failure to record or accurately maintain records. We can be as certain concerning the existence of any specified day in the year 1 B.C. as we are that the sun came up today. The most ancient of the exact sciences is astronomy, and it is because of astronomy that we can measure time. All peoples who have written history have been able to measure and define the earth's movements within rather exact limits. Consequently we are able, as our ancient ancestors were also, to define and measure what we mean by *time*.

Time is, in concept, continuous and subject to close examination. The understanding of the movement of the earth around the sun and of the rotation of the earth on its axis allows us to measure the year and the day with a precision that gives us great confidence in defining what we mean by the passage of time.

Our time is measured by the relative motions of spheres: the earth, the sun, the moon, the stars, and the planets. The measurement of time as we recognize it is unique to this world. Any other place in the universe has a different order of time. Most calendar systems evolved on this earth have used one, two, or all three of the natural cycles of time given by the movements of the earth, the sun, and the moon.

The first and most important unit of our time is the day, the natural period of rotation of the earth about its axis. The Sumerians took that period of rotation and, by dint of their duodecimal system, divided it evenly into twenty-four hours. In our own time, the day continues to be by definition exactly twenty-four hours.

The movement of the earth around the sun gives us the seasons and, independent of the cycle of day and night, the second unit of our time: the year. The solar year is measured precisely by reckoning the number of times the earth revolves on its axis between the occurrence of one spring equinox and the following spring equinox. (An equinox is that time when the rays of the sun are perpendicular to the equator, thereby making the length of night and day equal in all parts of the earth.) The length of the solar year is currently equivalent to 365 days, 5 hours, 48 minutes, and 46 seconds. The solar year, measured in days, is decreasing by about 5.3 seconds per 1,000 years.[2]

The solar year is about 1 minute and 14 seconds less than 365.25 days. This fact gave rise to the Gregorian calendar reform of the sixteenth century. Few people using our current calendar (established by the Gregorian reform) understand that three times every four hundred years there are otherwise regularly scheduled leap years that are not given an extra day. The year 1900, accordingly, was not given an extra day. This fine adjustment, which is not scheduled to be made again until the year 2100, is related to the Gregorian calendar's attempt to keep our reckoning of days of the year within the cycle of the seasons.

The shadow of the moon gives us the third unit that men have used to measure time: the lunar cycle. The phases of the moon are subject to the gravitational forces of earth and the sun. This results in recurrent slight variations in the length of the lunar cycle. An average approximation of this cycle is 29 days, 12 hours, 44 minutes, and 2.78 seconds

8

(29.5306 days). Although the Gregorian calendar does not take into consideration the cycle of the moon, the moon's movement has given to men, from the earliest times, a third important cycle for measuring time. Most Middle East and Far East cultures still measure the passage of time by lunar cycles.

The earth's rotational movement does not evenly divide the solar year or the lunar cycle. This creates a problem for all calendar systems: How does one divide larger units of time so that days can be understood to have some meaningful relation to each other? The problem is often solved by associating groups of days with other natural cycles of time, such as the seasons and the phases of the moon. But this solution is somewhat artificial because one cannot easily measure lunar months or solar years in multiples of whole days.

Chronology, the study of time as it relates to history, involves simple arithmetic; dates are either consistent with each other or they are not. The main problem, however, is not the mathematics but the determination of the timing of secular and sacred events from sources that use different calendars or points of reference. In ancient history there are generally two sources for chronological research: (1) the beginning and end of the reigns of kings and rulers, as well as the timing of important events associated with particular kingships or periods of government, and (2) astronomical events, such as solar and lunar eclipses and the relative positions of heavenly bodies. Science often provides a definitive answer for the timing of an event that actual observation associated with astronomical phenomena. Celestial mechanics are exact and not subject to the errors that can otherwise arise from an interpretation of dates recorded with different points of reference.

The chronology of ancient history is closely tied to the rise and fall of empires, kings, and rulers. It is recorded in sometimes unfamiliar calendars with uncertain points of reference. It can be confusing and perplexing for even the experts. It often leads to contradictory or ambiguous results. Nevertheless, history is recorded in the flow of time that we understand and measure. There is only one correct sequence of sacred and secular events. Acknowledging this state of affairs, I believe that it is possible to show that a young prophet one hundred and fifty years ago through the gift and power of God identified with remarkable accuracy a direct chronological link between two important religious events.

CHAPTER 3

The Birth of Christ

". . . the coming of our Lord and Savior Jesus Christ in the flesh." (D&C 20:1.)

"For unto you is born this day in the city of David a Saviour, which is Christ the Lord." (Luke 2:11.)

In our reckoning of time, I believe that Jesus of Nazareth was born of Mary in Bethlehem of Judea on the night of April 5-6, 1 B.C. The Bible, however, does not give enough information to determine this exact date. The New Testament relates at least five circumstances that are associated with Christ's birth: (1) Herod the Great is king of Judea, (2) Caesar Augustus is emperor of Rome, (3) Cyrenius (the Latin form is Quirinius) is governor of Syria, (4) shepherds are in the field, and (5) a new star appears. In addition, Luke gives a year in the reign of Tiberius Caesar during which John the Baptist began his ministry, and the approximate age Christ had reached when John baptized him.

Scholars have examined the references to the birth of Christ for centuries. Each biblical verse has received careful

11

and thoughtful consideration. Unfortunately, the few secular records of the first century make it difficult to determine in our own calendar the time of Christ's birth. The weight of evidence produced so far by traditional scholarship suggests that Christ was born sometime during 7-5 B.C.[3] Those years are at variance with the chronology presented in this study. Those years are also difficult, if not impossible, to correlate with the time of the beginning of the Lord's ministry as found in Luke 3:1-2 and with the length of Christ's life as recorded in 3 Nephi 8:5.

One can be certain that any specific date or year identified as being associated with the birth of Christ will cause contention among scholars. My intent is not to add to that contention, but to show how the modern revelation concerning the significance of April 6 is in perfect harmony with other sacred writings. With this in mind, let us briefly review some of the biblical references to the birth of Christ.

Herod the Great of Judea

"Now when Jesus was born in Bethlehem of Judea in the days of Herod the king. . . ." (Matthew 2:1.)

". . . for they are dead which sought the young child's life." (Matthew 2:20.)

Matthew clearly states that Herod the Great was alive at the time of Christ's birth. The king was an old man who was tormented by a life of evil works and by "an intolerable itching over all the surface of his body."[4] By the time of Christ's birth Herod the Great had murdered, among others, his wife, three of his sons, his wife's brother, and his wife's grandfather. With that kind of record, is it any wonder that Herod sought to destroy the baby Jesus, or that the Holy Family fled to Egypt to await the death of the evil king?

12

The traditional approach in narrowing the limits of time for the birth of Christ is to first determine the likely time of the death of Herod the Great. Josephus, a Jewish historian who lived in the first century, gives by far the most information on the reign of Herod the Great, but much of his chronology (especially the length of the king's reign) is disputed by scholars. Josephus mentions among other things that Herod the Great died after an eclipse of the moon and before a Passover.[5] In their search for the year of the death of Herod the Great and the pivotal point of Christ's birth, most scholars have identified the eclipse of the moon on the night of March 12-13, 4 B.C. (Julian calendar), as the eclipse referred to by Josephus. This, of course, implies that Christ was born no later than March 4 B.C.[6] Contrary to what some have assumed, the lunar eclipse of 4 B.C. is not conclusive evidence. W. E. Filmer has identified two other lunar eclipses visible from Jerusalem that could satisfy Josephus's account.[7] One eclipse occurred on January 9, 1 B.C. (Julian calendar), and the other on December 29, 1 B.C. (Julian calendar). The second eclipse was visible when the moon rose over the eastern horizon of Jerusalem in the evening—a time when many people in Judea would have been awake to note the unusual phenomenon of a moon rising in eclipse. As early as the sixteenth century, Joseph Scaliger, the mastermind behind the Gregorian calendar reform and the Julian period used by astronomers, decisively maintained that the death of Herod the Great was connected with a 1 B.C. eclipse.[8]

The death of Herod the Great is an important factor in trying to determine the time of Christ's birth. There remains, nevertheless, doubt about the year of his death. It is premature to claim conclusively that Herod died sometime before the Passover of 4 B.C. My own preference, which is not based on any independent analysis of existing historical sources, is to put the death of Herod the Great in the early spring of A.D. 1, after the lunar eclipse of December 29, 1 B.C. This, of course, allows for an April birth of Christ in the year 1 B.C. I recognize that most scholars are prepared to dispute the likelihood of a 1 B.C. birth, but in making their case against such a likelihood, such scholars will likely rely on the writings of Josephus—writings that can be ambiguous and inconsistent.

Emperor of Rome

"And it came to pass in those days, that there went out a decree from Caesar Augustus, that all the world should be taxed." (Luke 2:1.)

The Messiah came into a Roman world. The inheritance of Abraham, Isaac, and Jacob was governed by Roman law, taxed in Roman coin, and policed by Roman centurions. The governors reckoned time from the founding of Rome, the Eternal City on the River Tiber.

Caesar Augustus ruled as emperor of Rome from 27 B.C. to A.D. 14. These years place his reign well within any probable date for Christ's birth. No one has yet found another record that conclusively refers to the taxing (census) of all the world, a hyperbole for the Roman Empire, around the year of Christ's birth.[9] Luke 2:1, nevertheless, confirms that Augustus was the emperor of Rome at the beginning of the Christian era.

Governor of Syria

"And this taxing was first made when Cyrenius was governor of Syria." (Luke 2:2.)

A lot of research and analysis has been spent on the twelve words of Luke 2:2. Luke gives a secular reference for the time of the birth of Christ when he writes that Quirinius (Cyrenius), a Roman senator, was governor of Syria. There seems to be agreement among the experts that

14

P. Sulpicus Quirinius was governor of Syria in A.D. 6-7,[10] but there is no hard historical evidence to support the notion that he was legate or governor of Syria any time before A.D. 6. Jack Finegan proposes the possibility that Quirinius may have been governor of Syria for the first time in 4-1 B.C.[11] Raymond Brown in his listing of Syrian legates identifies C. Sabinus or L. C. Piso as possible candidates for the period of 4-1 B.C.[12] Some have suggested that Quirinius may have been the Syrian legate on two different occasions, the first occurring at the turn of the first century. There continues to be uncertainty among historians as to the identity of the governor of Syria in 4-1 B.C. This uncertainty is removed for the periods 9-6 B.C. and 6-4 B.C., when C. Sentius Saturninus and P. Quinctilius Varus were, respectively, governors of Syria.[13] So it should be noted that the consensus among biblical scholars that Christ was born sometime between 7 and 5 B.C. does not appear to be compatible with Luke 2:2.

Shepherds in the Field

"There were in the same country shepherds abiding in the field, keeping watch over their flock by night." (Luke 2:8.)

The biological rhythm of sheep, like that of other animals, is influenced by the seasons of the year. The lambing season occurs in the spring. In the Middle East sheep drop their lambs within a period of about two weeks from late March to early April. During this season the flocks require the constant attention of their keepers. During lambing, for the safety of their flocks and preservation of the newborn, shepherds keep careful watch over their sheep. At no other time in the year are shepherds more closely tied to their flocks.

In summer and fall, one may expect that the flocks are

15

under watch by night, but this watch is not as demanding as during the lambing season. During these seasons one man, or even a boy, could take the night watch while the rest of the shepherds slept. Only in the spring, during the lambing season, are shepherds anxious about the lives of their sheep—so anxious that they keep watch over their flocks throughout the night.

Many pilgrims in Bethlehem during the middle of winter have been struck by the coldness of the Judean nights. At that time of year the hills and valleys are in the grip of frost, and there are few, if any, shepherds keeping watch over their flocks by night. The sheep are protected from the cold in simple shelters, or have been taken south to the desert. In the winter the shepherds of Judea look forward to the coming of spring so that they can return with their flocks to the green grass of the hills. Judean shepherds can be found in the fields keeping watch over their sheep any time from mid-March to early November, but the one time of the year during which their round-the-clock attention is required is the lambing season.

Considering how the seasons of the year affect the behavior of the sheep and the shepherds, it seems reasonable to conclude that the shepherds in the hills of Judea would be "keeping watch over their flocks by night" (Luke 2:8) in the spring of the year and that, therefore, spring was a likely time for the birth of Christ. The night of April 5-6 falls during the lambing season. Was it not on that night that the angelic choir sang to the shepherds: "Glory to God in the highest, and on earth peace, good will toward men"? (Luke 2:14.)

New Star Appears

"Saying, Where is he that is born King of the Jews? for we have seen his star in the east, and are come to worship him." (Matthew 2:2.)

16

". . . and, lo, the star, which they saw in the east, went before them, till it came and stood over where the young child was." (Matthew 2:9.)

"And behold, there shall a new star arise, such an one as ye never have beheld; and this also shall be a sign unto you." (Helaman 14:5.)

"And it came to pass also that a new star did appear, according to the word." (3 Nephi 1:21.)

For centuries astronomers have attempted to identify the star that heralded the birth of Christ.[14] Some astronomers have speculated that the new star could have been a nova or a supernova. A nova is a very distant star that explodes, giving out a great deal of light. A supernova can be a hundred million times brighter than a middle-sized star, which may make it appear to be brighter than the moon in the night sky. About a dozen novae are observed by astronomers each year, but novae visible to the naked eye are rare. It is quite possible, however, that the new star mentioned in the Bible and the Book of Mormon was a supernova.

Another explanation of the Star of Bethlehem was first made in the early seventeenth century by Johannes Kepler, the renowned German astronomer and mathematician. He observed the conjunction of Jupiter and Saturn on December 17, 1603.[15] Being very impressed with the spectacular sight, he calculated that the two bright planets also came together in 7 B.C. Since then other persons have speculated that the Star of Bethlehem could have been the triple conjunction of Saturn and Jupiter in the constellation of Pisces during October of 7 B.C.

The scriptures, reflecting contemporary observation, refer to a new star, *not* to the temporary conjunction of two

17

planets, a phenomenon that the ancients understood. Astronomers of the near East and pre-Columbian America followed the movements of the planets and would not have identified the conjunction of Saturn and Jupiter as a new star. Herod's surprise at being told of the star by the magi suggests that the Star of Bethlehem may not have been particularly large or spectacular. At this time it seems best to conclude that astronomy neither confirms nor refutes the appearance of a new star on the night of Christ's birth.

Additional Evidence from Luke

> "Now in the fifteenth year of the reign of Tiberius Caesar, Pontius Pilate being governor of Judea, and Herod being tetrarch of Galilee, and his brother Philip tetrarch of Ituraea and of the region of Trachonitis, and Lysanias the tetrarch of Abilene, Annas and Caiaphas being the high priests, the word of God came unto John the son of Zacharias in the wilderness." (Luke 3:1-2.)

There are few references in the New Testament that seem as easy to fix in time as the above scripture. Most historians identify August 17, A.D. 14 (Julian calendar), as the beginning of the reign of Tiberius Caesar, the second emperor of Rome.[16] Luke tells us that John the Baptist began his ministry in the fifteenth year of the reign of Tiberius. This suggests that sometime between A.D. 27 and A.D. 29 John came "into all the country about Jordan, preaching the baptism of repentance for the remission of sins." (Luke 3:3.) This information is useful but not conclusive in determining the time of our Lord's ministry as well as the year of his birth.

Luke gives us another important reference from which it is possible to approximate the time of the birth of Christ.

18

We read: "Now when all the people were baptized, it came to pass, that Jesus also being baptized, and praying, the heaven was opened, And the Holy Ghost descended in a bodily shape like a dove upon him, and a voice came from heaven, which said, Thou art my beloved Son; in thee I am well pleased. And Jesus himself began to be about thirty years of age, being (as was supposed) the son of Joseph." (Luke 3:21-23.)

The Gospel of Luke tells us that John was baptizing in the waters of Jordan "in the fifteenth year of the reign of Tiberius Caesar" (Luke 3:1), and that during John's ministry "Jesus himself began to be about thirty years of age." (Luke 3:23.) These two references make it possible to approximate the year of Christ's birth. Historians recognize Tiberius as an important figure in the history of Rome and are able to define within a tolerance of at least two years the timing of the fifteenth year of his reign. Luke records that Christ was almost thirty when he was baptized. These chronological references would support 1 B.C. as the year of the birth of our Lord. On the other hand, these references from Luke contradict the popular thesis that Christ was born sometime in 7-5 B.C.

Change in Approach

The last few pages have briefly reviewed the New Testament references to the birth of Christ. Unfortunately, the Bible by itself does not give enough information to specify either the date or the year of the birth of Christ. Biblical scholarship has not yet produced the exact timing of Christ's birth. This situation is not the failure of intense and demanding research, but stems from a lack of specific references in the Bible or other Old World writings that can unambiguously be associated with time as we recognize and measure it. One may sort, collate, and correlate biblical chronology in a thousand or more pages and it is still

19

doubtful whether any firm consensus would be reached among the scholars concerning the timing of the birth of Christ.

Latter-day scriptures open a new door to our understanding of ancient times. I accept the first verse of the twentieth section of the Doctrine and Covenants as having a specific and literal meaning. I ask the reader to assume, at least for the sake of the presentation, that April 6 has historic and religious significance. Toward the end of this study is a summary of the harmony of that date—a harmony based on literally thousands of calculations. One can only find this harmony when he considers the Bible together with the Book of Mormon and the Doctrine and Covenants. Without latter-day scriptures there is not enough specific information to determine the day of Christ's birth. Without the translations and revelations of Joseph Smith there is no specific point in time to which one can fix the birth of the Savior. I believe that with modern scriptures we can examine more completely the pivotal point of our time, the beginning of the Christian era, the birth of our Lord and Savior, Jesus Christ.

Table 1 Birth of Christ as Observed in Palestine in 1 B.C.

Event	Day of Week	Julian Calendar	Gregorian Calendar	Judean Method of Reckoning[1]	Galilean and Pharisee Method of Reckoning[2]
Spring equinox, 3 P.M.	Monday	March 22	March 20		
	Tuesday	March 23	March 21		
Moonless night Astronomical new moon, 1:49 P.M.[3]	Wednesday	March 24	March 22		
At sunset a thin lunar crescent appears above western horizon in Jerusalem[4]	Thursday	March 25	March 23	Sunset for Sadducees and Judeans marks beginning of day and month of Nisan.	Nisan 1 Sunrise for Galileans and Pharisees marks beginning of day and month of Nisan.
(Upon verified sighting of the lunar crescent, the Sanhedrin sanctifies the new month with the sounding of silver trumpets from the temple wall and lighting of fires on tops of hills.)					
	Friday	March 26	March 24	Nisan 1	Nisan 2
Jewish Sabbath	Saturday	March 27	March 25	Nisan 2	Nisan 3
	Sunday	March 28	March 26	Nisan 3	Nisan 4
	Monday	March 29	March 27	Nisan 4	Nisan 5
	Tuesday	March 30	March 28	Nisan 5	Nisan 6
	Wednesday	March 31	March 29	Nisan 6	Nisan 7

(The Law requires all healthy male Jews over twelve years of age and living within ninety miles of the temple to celebrate Passover in Jerusalem. In addition, Caesar Augustus has decreed that all the world should be taxed.)

Event	Day				
Jewish Sabbath	Saturday	April 3	April 1	Nisan 9	Nisan 10
	Sunday	April 4	April 2	Nisan 10	Nisan 11
	Monday	April 5	April 3	Nisan 11	Nisan 12
	Tuesday	April 6	April 4	Nisan 12	Nisan 13
Astronomical full moon, 2:21 P.M. In afternoon Paschal lambs are slain at temple for Galileans and Pharisees. Joseph and Mary arrive in Bethlehem, five miles south of Jerusalem	Wednesday	April 7	April 5	Nisan 13	Nisan 14
Birth of Jesus Christ occurs sometime during this night[5]				Sunset marks beginning of Nisan 14	Galileans and Pharisees eat Passover meal at sunset

(Within a tolerance of a few minutes, 12:00 midnight is exactly 1,830 years removed from 8:00 A.M. Jerusalem Time, April 6, 1830, or 1:00 A.M. Eastern Standard Time, April 6, 1830)

Event	Day				
In afternoon Paschal lambs are slain at temple for Sadducees and Judeans	Thursday	April 8	April 6	Nisan 14 — Sunset marks beginning for Sadducees and Judeans of Passover, Nisan 15	Nisan 15
Passover and the first day of the Feast of Unleavened Bread	Friday	April 9	April 7	Nisan 15	Nisan 16
Jewish Sabbath and First Fruits of the Harvest	Saturday	April 10	April 8	Nisan 16	Nisan 17
	Sunday	April 11	April 9	Nisan 17	Nisan 18
	Monday	April 12	April 10	Nisan 18	Nisan 19
	Tuesday	April 13	April 11	Nisan 19	Nisan 20
	Wednesday	April 14	April 12	Nisan 20	Nisan 21
Circumcision of the Christ child. Seventh and last day of the Feast of Unleavened Bread among Judeans and Sadducees[7]	Thursday	April 15	April 13	Nisan 21	Nisan 22

Note: Unless otherwise specified, all times are expressed as they would have been recorded in the time zone of Jerusalem.

CHAPTER 4

The Passover and
The Birth of Christ

Table 1 shows the correlation among four calendars during the spring of 1 B.C. The Julian and at least two different Jewish calendars were in use at the time, as was the familiar cycle of the seven-day week. The Gregorian calendar was not used nor known in the first century. That calendar was introduced in the mid-sixteenth century by Pope Gregory XIII, and has since become the most common calendar throughout the world. The Gregorian calendar dates are calculated as if that calendar had existed during the time of Christ's birth. Our calendar, the Gregorian calendar, would have identified the night of Christ's birth as April 5-6, 1 B.C. The Julian calendar places the birth on April 7-8, 1 B.C.

The dating of Christ's birth in Jewish calendars of the first century is unexpectedly symbolic. The birth of Christ was recognized by the normative Jews as having occurred on the night of Nisan 14, a time when the Galileans and Pharisees were most likely celebrating the Passover meal. The Passover was celebrated during the time of the full moon in the spring. It was, and continues to be, an important celebration during the Jewish year. Some pious Jews consider Passover an important time in the future chronology of Israel. The Passover table currently includes a place and cup of wine reserved for Elijah, whom the Jews expect some day to return for the eating of the Passover meal, an event that the Latter-day Saints believe occurred on Passover, April 3, 1836, at the Kirtland Temple. (See D&C 110:12-16.)

The fixing of the Jewish Passover month to the spring lunar cycle of 1 B.C. shows that Christ came into the world on Nisan 14—the same day, in the calendar of the Galileans, in which he ate the Last Supper, and the same day, in the calendar of the Judeans, on which he died. The birth of Christ at the beginning of the Passover feast is of significance. In the reckoning of Deity this was not coincidental. The birth of the Messiah occurred at that time of the year when God's covenant with Israel was most remembered and honored by the children of Abraham, Isaac, and Jacob. The Messiah came to earth to redeem his people at a time when remembrance of Jehovah was uppermost in the minds of the children of Israel.

The Passover birth of Christ takes on greater meaning when we examine the writings of the Jews. According to Jewish literature, Isaac, the only son of Abraham and Sarah, was born on the first day of Passover and "at his birth the sun shone with unparalleled splendor, the like of which will only be seen at the time of the Messiah's coming."[17] The suggestion here is that the birth of Isaac was a prototype of the coming of the Messiah.

In addition, the *Midrash Rabbah*, a collection of rabbinic writings commenting on the Old Testament,[18] indicates that the Messiah would appear on Passover.[19] Exodus 12:42 states that Passover is "a night to be much observed unto the Lord" (a night of watching) and that it "is that night of the Lord to be observed of all the children of Israel in their generations." *Midrash Rabbah* focuses on this verse and asks the question, "Why does He call it a night of watching?"

25

The answer then follows: "Because, on that night, He performed great things for the righteous, just as He had wrought for Israel in Egypt. On that night, He saved Hezekiah, Hanniah and his companions, Daniel from the lions' den, and on that night Messiah and Elijah will be made great (will appear) . . . 'Let this (Passover) be a sign to thee; and whenever thou seest this sign, know that I will soon come back.' "[20]

Jewish tradition clearly links the coming of the Messiah to Passover. This tradition has deep historical roots and appears to be in perfect harmony with the revelation concerning April 6, 1830, it "being one thousand eight hundred and thirty years since the coming of our Lord and Savior Jesus Christ in the flesh." (D&C 20:1.)

At the time of Christ's birth hundreds of thousands, perhaps millions, of Jews were in Jerusalem to celebrate the Passover and renew their faith in the God of their fathers. At no other time during the year would Jerusalem be so crowded. The large crowds taxed the facilities of the city and suburbs.

Is it any wonder that Joseph and Mary were unable to find appropriate shelter? Bethlehem is about five miles south of the walls of Jerusalem. The overflow Passover crowds had apparently filled even the city of David. Luke tells us that Joseph and Mary were in Bethlehem because of Caesar's census. It also appears that Joseph was commanded by his religion to be at Jerusalem for the celebration of Passover.

While in Bethlehem, Mary gave birth to the Christ child at the beginning of Israel's Passover feast, at a time that in her calendar, would bring great sorrow and grievous suffering thirty-three years later; and at a time that, in our calendar, would witness the restoration of the kingdom of God 1,830 years later. What great and marvelous things are associated with the birth of Christ!

Figure 1. Relative positions of the sun, moon, and earth at midnight during the night of Christ's birth.

Note: The astronomical full moon is calculated to have occurred at 1:49 P.M. Jerusalem Time. At midnight the moon appears full and is almost directly over Jerusalem.

Sun

Earth

Moon

Jerusalem

Table 2 Birth of Christ as Observed in America

Event	Time		Day of Week	Julian Calendar	Gregorian Calendar	New Nephite Calendar
Samuel the Lamanite prophesies that the sign of Christ's birth will be given in five years[1]	Spring 6 B.C.	End of the eighty-sixth year of the reign of the judges[2]				
	Spring 1 B.C.	Commencement of the ninety-second year of the reign of the judges[3]				
Spring equinox, 6 A.M.			Monday	March 22	March 20	
Astronomical new moon, 4:49 A.M.[4]			Wednesday	March 24	March 22	
New lunar crescent visible at sunset over western horizon			Wednesday	March 24	March 22	
			Thursday	March 25	March 23	
			Friday	March 26	March 24	
			Saturday	March 27	March 25	
			Sunday	March 28	March 26	
			Monday	March 29	March 27	
			Tuesday	March 30	March 28	
			Wednesday	March 31	March 29	
			Thursday	April 1	March 30	
			Friday	April 2	March 31	
			Saturday	April 3	April 1	

Day	Event		
Sunday		April 4	April 2
Monday	Nephi prays mightily to the Lord that his people not be destroyed because of their belief in the prophecies[5]	April 5	April 3
	(The unbelievers set aside a day—Wednesday, April 5, in the Gregorian calendar—on which all those who believe in the prophecy should be put to death unless the sign of Christ's birth is given)		
Tuesday	Sun goes down, but there is no darkness. Night is as light as midday, and the lives of the believers are saved	April 6	April 4
Wednesday	Astronomical full moon, 7:21 A.M.	April 7	April 5
	As measured in the New World, the birth of Jesus Christ occurs on this day		1st day / 1st month / 1st year
	(Within a tolerance of a few minutes 3:00 P.M. is 1,830 solar years from 1 A.M. Eastern Standard Time, April 6, 1830; 3:00 P.M. is the same as midnight Jerusalem Time)		

Note: Unless otherwise specified, all times are nine hours west of Jerusalem time

CHAPTER 5

The Book of Mormon Account of Christ's Birth

The followers of Christ in America believed in the exactness of the prophecies given through God's oracles. They were convinced that Samuel the Lamanite spoke under the influence of the Holy Spirit in the spring of 6 B.C. when he declared from the wall of the city of Zarahemla: "Behold, I give unto you a sign; for five years more cometh, and behold, then cometh the Son of God to redeem all those who shall believe on his name. And behold, this will I give unto you for a sign at the time of his coming; for behold, there shall be great lights in heaven, insomuch that in the night before he cometh there shall be no darkness, insomuch that it shall appear unto man as if it was day." (Helaman 14:2-3.)

When Samuel the Lamanite came to a city filled with unbelievers, scorners, and mockers, and told them that the Son of God would be born in five years, they marked the date in their calendars and began to count the days. The unbelievers fully expected that the prophecy would not be fulfilled. This, they thought, would give them greater reason to doubt the words of other prophets. The believers initially felt the promptings of the Spirit and looked forward to the day of promise.

"But behold, they did watch steadfastly for that day and that night and that day which should be as one day as if there were no night, that they might know that their faith had not been vain.

"Now it came to pass that there was a day set apart by the unbelievers, that all those who believed in those traditions should be put to death except the sign should come to pass, which had been given by Samuel the prophet." (3 Nephi 1:8-9.)

As the years went by, the explicit prophecy became threatening—especially to those whose faith, once strong, had begun to wane. The believers made no effort to redefine or reinterpret the clear, unambiguous prophecy so as to avoid the possibility that the sign might not be given. They accepted the prophecy completely and literally. Knowing this, the nonbelievers put the followers of Christ in the difficult position of choosing between their lives and their faith. Those faithful members must have felt a greatly increased awareness of time as they waited for the appointed day in April of 1 B.C. Their worship services on the Sabbath before the sign of Christ's birth were probably more devout than usual.

In reconstructing the drama of that day, one is amazed at the faith of those early followers of Christ. They knew that time was measurable and had meaning to God. They accepted without qualification the prophecies of holy men, and they waited with true devotion for the sign of Christ's birth. This sign had such great meaning to them that they were willing to place their lives on the altar as a test of its fulfillment.

Nephi, the grandson of Helaman and leader of the believers, cried unto God on behalf of his people who were in danger of being destroyed because of their faith. As he was praying he heard the voice of the Lord: "Lift up your head

31

and be of good cheer; for behold, the time is at hand, and on this night shall the sign be given, and on the morrow come I into the world, to show unto the world that I will fulfill all that which I have caused to be spoken by the mouth of my holy prophets." (3 Nephi 1:13.)

The sign of Christ's birth was a great event in the chronology of the Nephites. The lives of the faithful had been saved from destruction. Many of the nonbelievers accepted the message of the prophets, repented, and joined the ranks of the Church members. The sign had such a profound influence that the Nephites began a new calendar count. The normal reckoning of time was interrupted by the birth of Christ, and the Nephites began a new reckoning, marking the meridian of time and the beginning of a new age.

From Table 2 we observe that the astronomical full moon was visible over America during the night preceding the birth of Christ. The Book of Mormon states that there were to be "great lights in heaven" (Helaman 14:3) but does not indicate the nature or source of the light.

Isaiah 30:26 says that "the light of the moon shall be as the light of the sun." Jewish tradition has considered these words to be related to the advent of the Messiah. Solomon ben Isaac Rashi, a leading Jewish commentator on the Bible and Talmud in the eleventh century,[21] stated that in the time of the Messiah "there will be in the world only the brilliance of splendour and the sight of the Holy Spirit. In the days of the Messiah the light of the moon shall be as the light of the sun."[22] Astronomical calculations indicate that the night before Christ's birth was a night of a full moon, and the Book of Mormon relates that at the setting of the sun in normal course there was yet "no darkness in all that night, but it was as light as though it was mid-day." (3 Nephi 1:19.) Does this not partially fulfill the Messianic expectations of the Jews?

Figure 1 shows the relative positions of the earth and the moon at midnight during the night of Christ's birth in

Bethlehem of Judea. The earth revolved around the sun 1,830 times between midnight, Jerusalem Time, April 6, 1 B.C. (Gregorian calendar), and 1 A.M. Eastern Standard Time, April 6, 1830, the day of the restoration of the Church of Jesus Christ.

Figure 1 also illustrates that at the time of Christ's birth the eastern hemisphere was dark while the western hemisphere was exposed to the sun. The Book of Mormon affirms this by stating that for the people of America Christ's birth occurred during the day. ". . . the time is at hand, and on this night shall the sign be given, and on the morrow come I into the world . . ." (3 Nephi 1:13.)

"And it came to pass that the sun did rise in the morning again, according to its proper order, and they knew that it was *the day that the Lord should be born,* because of the sign which had been given." (3 Nephi 1:19. Italics added.)

These references to a daylight birth of Christ, assuming the historical accuracy of the biblical account, enhance the credibility of the assertion that the records from which the Book of Mormon were derived were historical records of a people living at that time on the western hemisphere.

CHAPTER 6

The Meridian of Time

"And it came to pass that Enoch looked; and from Noah, he beheld all the families of the earth; and he cried unto the Lord, saying: When shall the day of the Lord come? When shall the blood of the Righteous be shed, that all they that mourn may be sanctified and have eternal life?

"And the Lord said: It shall be in the meridian of time, in the days of wickedness and vengeance." (Moses 7:45-46.)

Most people who have lived under the influence of Christianity divide the world's history and chronology between the events occurring before and those occurring after the birth of Christ. When the Pearl of Great Price indicates that Christ's first advent came in the meridian of time, it states the obvious truth that that advent was the turning point of human history. On Mount Sinai Moses saw in vision that Adam had been commanded to teach his children of Jesus Christ, "a righteous Judge, who shall come in the meridian of time." (Moses 6:57.) This scriptural statement may be more meaningful and profound than its first reading indicates.

There exists a strong tradition in the writings of the Jews that the history of man's earthly experience can be placed within the framework of seven thousand years, a week of seven days wherein each day is one thousand years.[23] This view of time is not only significant to the manner in which religious Jews observe events, but is also of significance to the Latter-day Saints. In the dispensation of the fulness of time, the Lord has made it clear through the Prophet Joseph Smith that this earth's "continuance, or its temporal existence" is placed in a framework of seven thousand years, with the last thousand years being the millennial reign of Christ. (D&C 77:6, 10.)

Ancient and modern scriptures indicate that a week of seven days is a division of time sanctified by the Lord. He created the world in six days and rested on the seventh day. He commanded Moses in the wilderness to remember the Sabbath and keep it holy. (Exodus 20:8.) Over the centuries reflective and pious observance of the weekly Sabbath has literally preserved the soul and spirit of a people who could often have been dispirited, and has healed the grievous wounds inflicted by hostile neighbors. The observance of the Sabbath over the last two thousand years gives rise to a cycle of work and rest that permits us today to identify since the first century any Sabbath, and any day before the Sabbath—including the Friday on which Christ died—as having a certain, dependably fixed relation to any other day.

For good reason God sanctified the seventh day; and for equally good reason were anniversaries, particularly the anniversaries of the birth of mere mortals (such as emperors, who commanded worship of their birthdays), shunned by the pious or relegated to a secondary role. Yearly observances of the recurring and miraculous events of sowing, harvesting, and the coming of new life were not inappropriate, but paled into insignificance beside the weekly celebration of the Lord's day, the great symbol of the covenant

35

that bound God to Israel, of which God said: "It is a sign between me and the children of Israel." (Exodus 31:17.)

The lunar month also competed with the week as a model for the timing of recurring ritual. At the time of Christ there were several Jewish sects, each following a ritual practice that they felt most completely satisfied the law of Moses. Among these sects were the Essenes, about whom Josephus, Pliny the Elder, and other historians wrote. More recently we have received from the Dead Sea Scrolls significantly more information about the practices and beliefs of a religious community that most likely consisted of Essenes.[24] The Dead Sea Scrolls have increased our understanding of the events and thinking of people in the Holy Land during the first century.

The land of Judea at the time of Christ was full of anticipation and expectation. Many Jews awaited the arrival of the Messiah and the redemption of Israel. Members of the Jewish sect near the Dead Sea at Qumran were faithfully waiting for the coming of the anointed one. These people had great respect for the flow and meaning of time. We read from their *Manual of Discipline:* "They must not deviate by a single step from carrying out the orders of God at the times appointed for them; they must neither advance the statutory times nor postpone the prescribed seasons."[25]

The calendar used in Qumran at the Dead Sea was different from the lunisolar calendar used by other Jews living in Palestine.[26] This religious community in the desert used a calendar based on the week. There is uncertainty about the exact operation of their calendar, but their year apparently had 52 weeks, or 364 days, and their day began at sunrise. The first day of each month for them was always a Wednesday. This meant that their Passover would also occur each year on a Wednesday.

Why would the Dead Sea Scroll sect have insisted on starting their years and months as well as observing their Passover on Wednesday—the fourth day? Was it because God created "two great lights" on the fourth day, "the greater light to rule the day, and the lesser light to rule the night"? (Genesis 1:16.) Did these dissident Jews want to start their months as well as their year on the fourth day of the week because that was the day on which the sun and the moon became visible during the creation? There is as yet no conclusive evidence why those people maintained, even in the face of death, a calendar based on the week.

The people of Qumran were in the desert waiting for an event to take place in the future, which they called "the time of visitation."[27] The covenantors of Qumran looked forward to the arrival of a prophet "like unto Moses." The Messianic hope of these people still burns as one reads their scrolls. The Qumran sect went to the desert to wait the passage of time, which they chose to measure differently than did the main body of the Jews. Did they start their year on Wednesday because they expected the Messiah to come on that day of the week?

When we examine Christ's birth we note that he came at a time that would have been recognized by the people of the Dead Sea Scrolls as Wednesday, and that could likely have been their Passover. (One should bear in mind that their days began at sunrise, as did those of the Pharisees and Galileans.) Curiously, as observed from the western hemisphere, the birth of the Messiah occurred during the midday of a Wednesday. The coming of the promised Christ occurred during the meridian of time in the meridian of the week.

There appears to be a harmony and precision in the timing of Christ's birth. The believers in the Judean desert at the turn of the first century were looking for harmony in God's time and for the coming of the promised Savior. It seems that that they would have recognized the night of April 5-6, 1 B.C., as a night of watching, a night of expectation, and a "time of visitation."

Table 3   The Crucifixion and the Resurrection of Christ and the Dating of Passover in A.D. 33

Event	Day of Week	Julian Calendar	Gregorian Calendar	Judean Method of Reckoning	Galilean and Pharisee Method of Reckoning
Astronomical new moon, 12:41 P.M.	Thursday	March 19	March 17		
A thin lunar crescent appears at sunset above the western horizon in Jerusalem	Friday	March 20	March 18	Sunset marks a new day and the new crescent identifies the beginning of Nisan, the month of Passover	Nisan 1 Sunrise marks beginning of day and month
	Saturday	March 21	March 19	Nisan 1	Nisan 2
Spring equinox, 2 P.M.	Sunday	March 22	March 20	Nisan 2	Nisan 3
	Monday	March 23	March 21	Nisan 3	Nisan 4
	Tuesday	March 24	March 22	Nisan 4	Nisan 5
	Wednesday	March 25	March 23	Nisan 5	Nisan 6
	Thursday	March 26	March 24	Nisan 6	Nisan 7
	Friday	March 27	March 25	Nisan 7	Nisan 8
	Saturday	March 28	March 26	Nisan 8	Nisan 9
The triumphal entry of Jesus into Jerusalem. Passion week begins	Sunday	March 29	March 27	Nisan 9	Nisan 10
	Monday	March 30	March 28	Nisan 10	Nisan 11
	Tuesday	March 31	March 29	Nisan 11	Nisan 12
	Wednesday	April 1	March 30	Nisan 12	Nisan 13
In afternoon Paschal lambs are slain at temple for Galileans and Pharisees	Thursday	April 2	March 31	Nisan 13	

				Nisan 14 begins at sunset	Galileans and Pharisees eat Passover meal at sunset
Christ eats the Last Supper with his apostles	Thursday	April 2	March 31		
The Redeemer suffers in Gethsemane	Thursday	April 2	March 31		Nisan 14
The trial, crucifixion, death, and burial of Christ	Friday	April 3	April 1	Nisan 14	Nisan 15
Astronomical full moon, 5:02 P.M.	Friday	April 3	April 1		
Passover and Sabbath: Jewish high day. Christ visits the spirit world	Saturday	April 4	April 2	Nisan 15	Nisan 16
Resurrection of the Savior. Jewish feast: First Fruits of the Harvest	Sunday	April 5	April 3	Nisan 16	Nisan 17

Note: Consult Table 1 for references on how these sequences are derived

Figure 2. Relative positions of the sun, moon, and earth at the time of Christ's death.

Note: Christ dies in the ninth hour (3:00 P.M. Jerusalem Time). The astronomical full moon occurred at about 5:00 P.M.

Sun

Earth

Moon

CHAPTER 7

The Passover and the Crucifixion

"Your lamb shall be without blemish, a male of the first year: ye shall take it out from the sheep, or from the goats. And ye shall keep it up until the fourteenth day of the same month: and the whole assembly of the congregation of Israel shall kill it in the evening." (Exodus 12:5-6.)

"And it shall come to pass, when your children shall say unto you, What mean ye by this service? That ye shall say, It is the sacrifice of the Lord's passover. . . . And the children of Israel went away, and did as the Lord had commanded Moses." (Exodus 12:26-28.)

"Therefore, it is expedient that there should be a great and last sacrifice; and then shall there be, or it is expedient there should be, a stop to the shedding of blood; then shall the law of Moses be fulfilled; yea, it shall be all fulfilled, every jot and tittle, and none shall have passed away.

41

> *"And behold, this is the whole meaning of the law, every whit pointing to that great and last sacrifice; and that great and last sacrifice will be the Son of God, yea, infinite and eternal." (Alma 34:13-14.)*
>
> *"For even Christ our passover is sacrificed for us." (1 Corinthians 5:7.)*

The Gospels testify that Christ died on a cross. He died at a time of sacrifice. He died when the Jews sacrificed their Paschal lambs. He died when the children of Israel remembered the night of redemption when the angel of death passed over the Israelite houses in Egypt and smote the firstborn of the Egyptians. He died as the last great sacrifice, to atone for the sins of the world and to redeem the righteous.

The Gospels, fortunately, give great attention to the events surrounding the atonement, death, and resurrection of Christ. Almost one-third of the chapters in the Gospels contain the account of the last week of Christ's life. There is probably no week in the first century about which we have more information than that week during which Christ died. The events of that week are commemorated by more people than the events of any other week of the past. Every Sunday in thousands of congregations around the world millions of Latter-day Saints partake of the Lord's sacrament and remember the atoning sacrifice of Jesus Christ. Indeed, we are commanded by holy writ to remember always the events of the week of Christ's atonement, death, and resurrection.

A knowledge of the calendar traditions of the Jews at the time of Christ helps to identify the probable date of the last great sacrifice. The relation of the spring lunar cycle to the timing of Passover and the continuous seven-day week cycle over the last two thousand years indicate that Friday, April 3, A.D. 33 (Julian calendar), is a day that satisfies the New Testament account of the Crucifixion.

42

The Lord gave to Moses the Passover, which symbolized the offering of the Lamb of God and marked in the Hebrew calendar for one and a half millennia the time that Christ would die. Moses established this calendar according to the cycles of the sun and the moon and fixed the new moon in the spring as the "beginning of months" (Exodus 12:2), which was known as Abid and later became known among the post-exilic Jews as the month of Nisan (from Babylonian *Nisannu*). In the afternoon of the fourteenth day of that month the Paschal lamb was slain, and, after sunset, the Passover meal was eaten (Exodus 12).

During the time of Christ the Jews understood that the calendar and feasts given to them by Moses were essential to the practice of their religion. There were, however, differences of opinion as to what reckoning of time most completely satisfied the requirements of the law of Moses. The Essenes, as we have already noted, appeared to have followed a calendar based on the week. The normative Jews followed a lunisolar calendar but had differing views about when a day should begin. The Sadducees, the Jewish aristocracy, favored a reckoning of time in which the day went from sunset to sunset.[28] The Galileans and Pharisees appear to have followed a sunrise-to-sunrise scheme for setting the limits of their days. These differences may seem to be of little significance, but they become important in harmonizing the synoptic account of the Passover and Last Supper with the account of the Passover and crucifixion found in John.

At the time of Christ the Jews' lives orbited around the temple and the Sanhedrin. The temple was the place of sacrifice, and the Sanhedrin told the Jews when they should sacrifice. It would have been a mockery to God to offer an untimely sacrifice. The law of Moses gave them the order of the calendar and the method of marking the time of sacrifice.

The Judeans and Sadducees most likely determined the beginning of each month by the direct observation of a thin lunar crescent over Jerusalem in the western sky just after sunset. At that time the Sanhedrin sanctified the month and announced its beginning with the sounding of temple trumpets and the lighting of fires on the tops of hills.[29]

In order to keep Passover in the spring, the Sanhedrin periodically inserted a thirteenth lunar month before Nisan. This intercalation of an extra month was apparently made by following the Metonic cycle of the Babylonians and Greeks or by observing astronomical conditions in Judea. The celebration of Passover was kept in the spring also to ensure that the barley—the first green heads of grain—would be ready for the feast of the firstfruits of the harvest. This feast followed Passover "on the morrow after the sabbath." (Leviticus 23:11.)

Both sacred and secular history emphasize that the sighting of the new moon in the spring would trigger the necessary preparations for the Passover among the Jewish people. The first day of Nisan for the Judeans and Sadducees seems to have begun in the evening when the crescent of the spring moon appeared above the western horizon. The beginning of the fifteenth day of Nisan for the Judeans and Sadducees occurred at sunset and marked for them the time for eating the Passover meal.

The first day of Nisan for the Galileans and the Pharisees seems to have been at sunrise after a moonless night—about twelve hours before the calendar commission of the Sanhedrin witnessed the crescent of the new moon. The Galileans and Pharisees would then count fourteen sunrises into the month of Nisan. On the afternoon of their fourteenth day, they would sacrifice their Passover lambs. These calendar traditions imply that the Galileans and Pharisees sacrificed their lambs exactly one day before the Judeans and Sadducees. This reckoning also suggests that the Galileans and Pharisees would eat their Passover meal a night before the Judeans and Sadducees.

Matthew, Mark, and Luke record that the Savior with his apostles ate the Passover meal the night before his

44

death.[30] There is no doubt that Christ considered the Last Supper his Passover meal. We read in Luke 22:14-16 the following: "And when the hour was come, he sat down, and the twelve apostles with him. And he said unto them, With desire I have desired to eat this passover with you before I suffer: For I say unto you, I will not any more eat thereof, until it be fulfilled in the kingdom of God."

All four Gospels testify that Christ died in the afternoon of the day following the night of his Last Supper. Moreover, John indicates that for those who sought to destroy Christ's life, the morning of Good Friday was a time before their eating of the Passover meal. John 18:28 states: "Then they led Jesus from Caiaphas unto the hall of judgment: and it was early; and they themselves went not into the judgment hall, lest they should be defiled; but that they might eat the passover."

There is no contradiction between the synoptic account of Christ's Passover meal and the account of John in which we learn that those who sought the life of Christ had not yet eaten the Passover meal even though the Savior and his apostles had. It appears that Christ and his disciples followed the practice of the Galileans in setting the beginning of the day at sunrise, and that those who sought to kill Christ followed the custom of the Judeans by fixing sunset as the beginning of their day. These different systems used among first century Jews resulted in two different nights for the eating of Passover.

In addition, the New Testament clearly indicates a sunrise-to-sunrise reckoning among the disciples of Christ. Matthew 28:1 states that the women came to the tomb "in the end of the sabbath, as it began to dawn toward the first day of the week." Acts 4:3 also suggests that sunrise marked for the apostles the beginning of the day.

The chronology of our Lord's ministry as found in the New Testament, particularly in the Gospel of Luke, points to the year A.D. 33 as the time of our Lord's death. In that year the seven-day week cycle and the fixing of the month of Nisan to the spring moon conform to the biblical account of the crucifixion and resurrection. At the very hour of Christ's sacrificial death, Judeans and Sadducees were slaying their Passover lambs at the temple. In addition, a close examination of the lunar cycle on Friday, April 3, A.D. 33 (Julian calendar), shows that the astronomical full moon occurred at the time Christ was taken from the cross. (See Table 3.)

The symbolism of sacrifice instituted by Moses was literally fulfilled, in Christ's death, in accordance with the ritual and timing Moses had prescribed.

Christ Visits the Spirit World

> "While this vast multitude waited and conversed, rejoicing in the hour of their deliverance from the chains of death, the Son of God appeared, declaring liberty to the captives who had been faithful." (D&C 138:18.)

> "By which also he went and preached unto the spirits in prison." (1 Peter 3:19.)

> "For for this cause was the gospel preached also to them that are dead, that they might be judged according to men in the flesh, but live according to God in the spirit." (1 Peter 4:6.)

After his death on Friday afternoon, Christ's disembodied spirit visited paradise to organize among the righteous dead a great ministry. During that brief time between his crucifixion and resurrection, the Lord "organized his forces and appointed messengers, clothed with power and authority, and commissioned them to go forth and carry the light of the gospel to them that were in darkness." (D&C 138:30.) The lifeless mortal body of our Savior rested in the tomb on the Jewish sabbath while his living

46

spirit appeared to the righteous dead "declaring liberty to the captives who had been faithful." (D&C 138:18.)

Those spirits who had been faithful to their testimony of Jesus while in the flesh rejoiced in the visit of Christ and in the hour of their redemption. The ministry that Christ began immediately following his death still goes on and will continue among the dead until all shall have a chance to hear the fulness of the gospel.

Firstfruits of the Resurrection

> "When ye be come into the land which I give unto you, and shall reap the harvest thereof, then ye shall bring a sheaf of the first-fruits of your harvest unto the priest: And he shall wave the sheaf before the Lord." (Leviticus 23:10-11.)
>
> "But now is Christ risen from the dead, and become the firstfruits of them that slept." (1 Corinthians 15:20.)
>
> "O death, where is thy sting? O grave, where is thy victory?" (1 Corinthians 15:55.)

The Lord, through Moses, commanded the children of Israel that when they had arrived in the Promised Land they were to offer the firstfruits of the field after Passover "on the morrow after the sabbath." (Leviticus 23:11.) At that time the high priest waved before the temple altar a sheaf of barley. On April 5, A.D. 33 (Julian calendar), the Jews celebrated the harvest of the firstfruits, and on that same day Christ rose from the dead and became "the first-fruits of them that slept." Once again we witness how the law of Moses gave to Israel a feast, fixed in the Hebrew calendar, that symbolized what was to have been one of the most important events in the history of the Lord's people and all others who would believe: the resurrection of the Christ, the confessed Messiah of Israel.

CHAPTER 8

The Length of Christ's Mortal Life as Recorded in Ancient America

"Now the Nephites began to reckon their time from this period when the sign was given, or from the coming of Christ." (3 Nephi 2:8.)

"And it came to pass in the thirty and fourth year, in the first month, on the fourth day of the month, there arose a great storm, such an one as never had been known in all the land." (3 Nephi 8:5.)

On the very day of Christ's birth the Nephites, a people descended from the colony of Lehi, began a new calendar count. This becomes an important fact as we examine their record to determine the length of the mortal life of their God, whom they identified as the Christ. The Nephite calendar began on the day of the birth of Christ. This means that the date of Christ's death, as measured in the

48

chronology of the Nephites, will show us the length of his mortal life. We have already determined that Friday, April 3, A.D. 33 (Julian calendar), satisfies the chronology of the crucifixion as given in the New Testament. This date is a point in time to which we can relate any other point in time. Once we know the length of Christ's mortal life we can then determine from his death date the day on which he was born.

The Book of Mormon gives us the length of Christ's life, but that measure of elapsed time is given in the reckoning of the people who lived in the western hemisphere during the first century. So we must first translate their reckoning into a specific number of days, and then simply count backwards from the hour of Christ's death to the time of his birth.

The Egyptian Calendar and the Book of Mormon

By their account, the people of Lehi had been influenced in their method of writing by Egyptian culture. Moroni, one of the last leaders of the people who preserved the inherited culture and its records, mentioned that he had written his record in reformed Egyptian. (Mormon 9:32.) In 600 B.C. Jerusalem was in the cultural orbit of Egypt, and it is probable that Lehi would have taken with him a calendar that was in general use at his time by the Egyptians. This supposition becomes even more persuasive as we closely and carefully examine the meaning of 3 Nephi 8:5 in the Book of Mormon, where the death of Christ is identified as occurring on the fourth day in the first month of the thirty-fourth year.

Scholars have worked diligently for more than a hundred years trying to piece together the various methods by which the ancient Egyptians measured time.[31] Though there are some points about their reckoning of time that are

49

still in doubt, there is general agreement about the basic structure of the Egyptian civil calendar. This calendar was used as early as 3000 B.C. and remained unchanged until about the beginning of the Christian era. It consisted of twelve months of thirty days each, plus five days outside the months. There was no effort to keep the civil year fixed to the seasons, nor was there any attempt to keep the lunar cycle of about twenty-nine and a half days within the months. Both the civil year and the months wandered through the solar cycle and the phases of the moon. In a century the Egyptian calendar showed the civil year moving slightly more than twenty-four days into the seasons. The new moon and full moon could occur on any day of any month without particular correlation.

The basic structure of the Egyptian civil calendar has something that few calendars in history have had: simplicity. Any peasant, or, for that matter, scholar, could understand the basic structure of the calendar. There were none of the rules we have for leap years. Time moved forward in the basic unit of days, and though the moon and the seasons were not in the calendar they were in nature for all to behold. Intercalation of days was too confusing to be bothered with: When should they be added? What about normal civil events occurring on leap days?

The 365-day year endured throughout Egypt for millennia. Even today the Copts of Egypt and Ethiopia, as well as the Perians and Parsees in India, continue to use a calendar based on the Egyptian calendar;[32] a system that has been in use longer than any other.

Archaeologists have determined that the most common calendars of pre-Columbian America had the same (constant) number of days as the Egyptian civil calendar. The civil calendars of the Maya and Aztec civilizations are simple in concept and function. Any schoolchild can master their basic form in a matter of minutes. First there is a day. Twenty days makes the next largest unit of time; we could call it a month. The year has eighteen of these twenty-day

50

months plus five days. The 365-day year with its five days standing outside any month is strikingly similar to the Egyptian civil calendar, and some scholars speculate that this pre-Columbian American calendar was influenced, either directly or indirectly, by the Egyptians. (The similarities between Central American and Egyptian cultures are not limited to the 365-day calendar count.)[33] The colony of Lehi, spoken of in the Book of Mormon, in its migration from the Near East to the western hemisphere, apparently brought with it at least one reckoning of time that it knew best—the civil calendar of the Egyptians.

Book of Mormon Death Date and Mesoamerican Calendars

We know from archaeological research that the Mesoamericans spent considerable effort and energy in measuring time. Indeed, available evidence suggests that the peoples of ancient America were perhaps more conscious of the flow of time than any people in history. The Mayans, in particular, have been called the children of time.[34] They were very careful in their measurement and observation of time's passage. All visible astronomical events, including the movements of the earth, the moon, the sun, the planets, and the stars, were measured and known to them. Mayan priests and astronomers would spend their whole lives recording, calculating, and debating the meaning of past, present, and future. For the Mayans the secrets of the world were to be found in the rhythms of time on earth and in the universe.

Archaeologists have established several characteristics of the calendar traditions of the ancient Americans.[35] The Mayan civil calendar has been identified as the base of other calendars known to have been used among the pre-Columbian inhabitants of Central America and Mexico. This

51

calendar divides the civil year into eighteen periods of twenty days, a reflection of the Mayan numbering system, with five additional days, which are outside the twenty-day months and are added to the end of each year. In other words, the Mayan civil calendar had a constant fixed length of 365 days. No effort was made to keep the civil calendar in pace with the seasons through a periodic intercalary adjustment, although the ancient inhabitants of America did understand that their civil year fell short of the solar year by a fraction of a day. Their astronomer-priests measured the length of the solar year with a greater exactness than is found in the Gregorian calendar—a calendar that was devised in the Western world not until the sixteenth century.

We read in the Book of Mormon that the people of America witnessed the signs of Christ's death "in the thirty and fourth year, in the first month, on the fourth day of the month." (3 Nephi 8:5.) The civil year used among pre-Columbian peoples was a non-intercalated 365-day year. This was the civil year of the Mayans, the Aztecs, and other peoples of Mexico, Central America, and South America. Using this same length for the year of the people spoken of in the book of 3 Nephi, we calculate that the period of 33 years and 4 days was 12,049 days ([33 × 365] + 4 = 12,049). This people in America counted 12,049 days, starting with the day of Christ's birth, to the day of his death. Having identified, in our own reckoning of time, the date of the Friday on which Christ was crucified (April 1, A.D. 33, Gregorian calendar), we are able to project backwards the 12,049 days of Christ's mortal life to find the date of his birth: the night of April 5-6, 1 B.C., a date that is exactly 1,830 solar years before April 6, 1830.[36]

CHAPTER 9

Restoration

"The rise of the Church of Christ in the last days, being one thousand eight hundred and thirty years since the coming of our Lord and Savior Jesus Christ in the flesh . . ." (D&C 20:1.)

"Which church was organized and established in the year of your Lord eighteen hundred and thirty, in the fourth month, and on the sixth day of the month which is called April." (D&C 21:3.)

"And verily, verily, I say unto you, that this church have I established and called forth out of the wilderness." (D&C 33:5.)

Tuesday, April 6, 1830, was a beautiful, clear day throughout the state of New York. It was the middle of a seven-day warm spell, the first period of springlike weather after the ice and snow of winter. It was as if Providence had blessed the day with sunny skies. Joseph Smith and his small group of followers felt on that day a special closeness to God. The warm temperatures, the clear skies, and the calm breezes made the appointed time and place seem to be in harmony with the will of God—a time and place appropriate for the restoration of his kingdom through the strength and power of the priesthood.

We turn to the journal of Joseph Smith to understand better the events of April sixth. He records: "We had received a commandment to organize the Church; and accordingly we met together for that purpose, at the house of Mr. Peter Whitmer, Sen., (being six in number,) on Tuesday, the sixth day of April, A.D., one thousand eight hundred and thirty. Having opened the meeting by solemn prayer to our Heavenly Father, we proceeded, according to previous commandment, to call on our brethren to know whether they accepted us as their teachers in the things of the Kingdom of God, and whether they were satisfied that we should proceed and be organized as a Church according to said commandment which we had received. To these several propositions they consented by a unanimous vote. I then laid my hands upon Oliver Cowdery, and ordained him an Elder of the 'Church of Jesus Christ of Latter-day Saints;' after which, he ordained me also to the office of an Elder of said Church. We then took bread, blessed it, and brake it with them; also wine, blessed it, and drank it with them. We then laid our hands on each individual member of the Church present, that they might receive the gift of the Holy Ghost, and be confirmed members of the Church of Christ. The Holy Ghost was poured out upon us to a very great degree—some prophesied, whilst we all praised the Lord, and rejoiced exceedingly. . . .

". . . after a happy time spent in witnessing and feeling for ourselves the powers and blessings of the Holy Ghost . . . we dismissed with the pleasing knowledge that we were now individually members of . . . 'The Church of Jesus Christ,' organized in accordance with commandments and revelations given by Him to ourselves in these last days."[37]

Joseph Smith clearly states that he had received from

God a commandment to establish once again the Church of Jesus Christ on a day identified through the spirit of prophecy and revelation. He accepted April 6 as having special significance in the chronology of God.

Three years after the restoration of the Church of Jesus Christ, Joseph Smith was in Jackson County, Missouri, and wrote that on Saturday, April 6, the members celebrated for the first time the anniversary of its restoration. It was the day before Easter, and that fact probably influenced Joseph Smith's thinking. In his journal he wrote about the linkage between the restoration of the Church and these other sacred events: (1) the coming into existence of the world, (2) Passover and the departure of the children of Israel from Egypt, (3) the vigil of the shepherds watching over their flocks by night at the time of Christ's birth, and (4) the death of Christ.[38] His writings clearly suggest that there is a direct chronological linkage between these events. He was certainly aware of the chronology and harmony of divine events, and he understood that the restoration of the Church was part of that scheme. He classified it as an event of spiritual significance on a par with the laying of the foundations of the earth, the exodus of Israel out of Egypt, and the birth, life, and death of Christ. He had at hand no calculations to show (as is true) that Christ's birth occurred on the same day, in the Hebrew calendar, as did his death. He could not plausibly have made this statement on any basis other than inspiration derived from the Creator—whose work it was to order the time and occurrence of events leading to the culmination of human history and the fulfillment of his will respecting his creation.

The nineteenth-century Mormons, whether in the East, the Midwest, or the West, continued to hold fast to their faith in the significance of April 6. Annual conferences of the Church were held on that day. Events of significance in connection with the erection of the Nauvoo Temple, the Salt Lake Temple, and the St. George Temple occurred on the anniversaries of the date of the Church's organization.

April 6 has become the single most important date in the history of the Church: not just because the Church was organized on that date, but because more significant historic events have occurred on that date than on any other day of the year. Latter-day Saints understand that April 6 has special historic significance for them.

April 6, 1830, acquires more significance and a deeper meaning as we reconstruct the close linkage of the restoration of the Church to the birth of Christ. The dispensation of the fulness of time was directly and carefully linked to the birth of Christ in the meridian of time.

Any great event in history becomes more significant—or at least more susceptible to appropriate commemoration—when we can identify the exact date on which it occurred. The restoration of the Church would have been a great event by any standards, be they those of believer, historian, or detractor, even if it had not been associated with the all-important birth of Christ and original proclamation of "good tidings of great joy." When we perceive that there exists an exact identification of the anniversary of Christ's birth with the restoration of the Church, there exists an even better reason regularly to recall and commemorate the significance of that date.

Both sacred and secular history exist within the dimensions of time and space. Indeed, the sacred record often tells of events that are yet to happen, of prophecies concerning the future. Joseph Smith had not only the prophetic power to see into the future, but was also blessed with power to identify important events in past spiritual history. The event marking the beginning of our age, the event to which the Western world relates all others, was identified by the young Prophet as having occurred exactly 1,830 years before April 6, 1830. Who among us would be so bold—unless God were with him? Our calendar is so sufficiently complex that only a few people can determine the days of the week on which their own birthdays occur. Man's recollection fades as a date is forgotten. The revelation dealing with the birth of Christ fixes a definite point in the long flow of time and says to us that this day, this precise moment in man's history, is a matter of vast significance. The restoration of the gospel in the fulness of time gives us another point of reckoning, an anchor for remembrance, and makes our understanding of time and our part in it more complete. There is a harmony of events in God's chronology, a sequence that he has ordained. God has revealed once again that which was lost and forgotten: the identification of that day on which was born "in the city of David, a Savior, which is Christ the Lord."

Christ's mortal life was enveloped in the dimensions of earth's time. He lived his life in the dimensions of time and space with which we are familiar and which speak to our own experience. The earth's motions give us our times and our seasons and the basis for relating any one of our experiences to others.

Through Joseph Smith in 1832 the power and purpose of the Lord in relation to human destiny were declared, with the sternly resounding conclusion: "He comprehendeth all things, and all things are before him. . . . He hath given a law unto all things, by which they move in their times and their seasons; And their courses are fixed, even the courses of the heavens and the earth." (D&C 88:41-43.) Whatever the public and private uncertainties of our time, we may be sure, if we will to believe, that God's purpose will be fulfilled: to bring to pass the immortality and eternal life of man.

Summary

Joseph Smith linked the restoration of the Church of Jesus Christ to the birth of our Savior. The New Testament records that Christ died on a Friday that coincided with the observance of Passover. The Book of Mormon records the length of Christ's life to the nearest day in the calendar of the ancient Americans. Keeping all these points in mind, let us enumerate the conditions that Joseph Smith would have to satisfy if without revelation he had independently identified April 6, 1830, as a day that is in harmony with the Bible and the Book of Mormon.

1. He would have to know the calendar traditions of the Jews at the time of Christ with respect to the lunar cycle and the solar year.

2. He would have to determine that the lunar crescent in the spring of A.D. 33 was first visible over Jerusalem after sunset on Friday March 20 (Julian calendar) marking for the Judeans the beginning of the first day of Nisan, the Jewish month of Passover.

3. He would have to identify Friday, April 3, A.D. 33 (Julian calendar) as a day compatible with the events surrounding the crucifixion.

4. He would have to identify the timing of Passover for the year 1 B.C. to determine a day that would satisfy a long-standing tradition among the Jews that the Messiah would appear on Passover.

5. He would have to understand that a basic element of calendar systems of ancient America is a fixed year of 365 days.

6. He would have to determine that from Wednesday, April 7, 1 B.C. (Julian calendar) to Friday, April 3, A.D. 33 (Julian calendar) is 12,049 days.

7. He would have to translate 12,049 days in a calendar of Mesoamerica as being 33 years and 4 days.

8. He would have to consider in his calculations the time difference between Jerusalem and America.

9. He would have to associate a particular night in Judea as being 1,830 solar years before April 6, 1830, which implies a knowledge of the length of the solar year within a tolerance of about twenty seconds.

It is beyond the realm of probability that a young man who had spent the first twenty-four years of his life in the rural districts of America could have calculated the astronomical and historical conditions that harmonize with the birth and death of Jesus Christ as recorded in the Bible, the Book of Mormon, and the Doctrine and Covenants. It is reasonable to conclude that the best scholars in the United States in 1830 would have found it difficult, if not impossible, to meet all the independent conditions that Joseph Smith satisfied when he announced that April 6, 1830, was the birthday of Jesus Christ.

The harmony of the April 6 date gives another testimony that Joseph Smith was a true messenger of the Lord Jesus Christ. The organization of The Church of Jesus Christ of Latter-day Saints was a great event in God's plan for this earth and its people. For this reason the anniversary of Christ's birth was chosen as appropriate for the establishment of his Kingdom in the latter days. The small group of believers meeting in the Whitmer home in the spring of 1830 was of little consequence in the eyes of the world. But the ultimate destiny of Christ's church is to fill the whole earth, with Christ himself at its head.

59

Table 4[1] Dates of Christ's Birth, Death, and Resurrection, and the Organization of The Church of Jesus Christ of Latter-day Saints

	Birth[2]	
	Jerusalem	America
Solar Years	0	
Days	0	
Julian Date[6]	1,721,155.48 ± .15	
Calendar Systems[7]		
Gregorian		
Year	1 B.C.	1 B.C.
Month	April	April
Day	5-6	5
Weekday	Wednesday-Thursday	Wednesday
Time	8:00 P.M.-3:00 A.M.	11:00 A.M.-6:00 P.
Julian		
Year	1 B.C.	1 B.C.
Month	April	April
Day	6-7 (7-8)	7 (6)
Hebrew		
Year	3760	
Month	Nisan	
Day	14	
Nephite		
Year		1st
Month		1st
Day		1st
Astronomical Data[8]		
Length of Solar Year	365.24231545 days	
New Moon		
Year	1 B.C.	
Month	March	
Day	24*	
Time	1:49 P.M.	
Full Moon		
Year	1 B.C.	
Month	April	
Day	7*	
Time	2:21 P.M.	

*Julian calendar dates
**Galilean day begins at sunrise. See Table 1

Death[3]		Resurrection[4]	Church Organization[5]
Jerusalem	America	Jerusalem	
			1,830
12,048.65			668,393.33
1,733,204.13		1,733,205.8	2,389,548.81
A.D. 33 April 1 Friday 3:00 P.M.	A.D. 33 April 1 Friday 6:00 A.M.	A.D. 33 April 3 Sunday morning	A.D. 1830 April 6 Tuesday
A.D. 33 April 3	A.D. 33 April 3	A.D. 33 April 5	
3793 Nisan 14 (15)**		3793 Nisan 16 (17)**	5590 Nisan 12
	34th 1st 4th		
			365.24220309 days
A.D. 33 March 19* 12:41 P.M.			A.D. 1830 March 24 12:50 P.M.
A.D. 33 April 3* 5:02 P.M.			A.D. 1830 April 8 5:31 A.M.

Notes

1. James E. Talmage, *Jesus the Christ* (Salt Lake City: Deseret Book Co., 1961), p. 104.

2. W. M. O'Neil, *Time and Calendars* (Sydney, Australia: Sydney University Press, 1975), p. 22.

3. Merrill F. Unger, *Unger's Bible Dictionary* (Chicago: Moody Press, 1966), p. 198. See also George A. Buutrick, ed., *The Interpreter's Dictionary of the Bible* (New York: Abingdon Press, 1962), pp. 599-603.

4. Josephus, *Wars of Jews*, book 1, chap. 32, par. 5.

5. Josephus, *Antiquities of the Jews*, XVII. vi. 4 (167), and ix. 3 (213).

6. For an excellent review of recent scholarship see Harold W. Hoehner, *Chronological Aspects of the Life of Christ* (Grand Rapids: Zondervan Publishing House, 1977).

7. W. E. Filmer, "The Chronology of the Reign of Herod the Great," *The Journal of Theological Studies*, 17(1966):283-84, 298. See refutation in T. D. Barnes, *The Journal of Theological Studies*, 19(1968):204-9.

8. Ernest L. Martin, "The Celestial Pageantry Dating of Christ's Birth," *Christianity Today*, vol. 21, no. 5 (December 3, 1976), p. 16.

9. Hoehner, *Chronological Aspects*, pp. 13-14, traces out the known censuses of the area in and around Palestine during the turn of the first century.

10. Raymond Brown, *Birth of the Messiah* (New York: Doubleday and Company, 1977), p. 550, appendix vii.

11. Jack Finegan, *Handbook of Biblical Chronology* (Princeton, N.J.: Princeton University Press, 1964), p. 235.

12. Brown, *Birth of Messiah*, p. 550.

13. Ibid.

14. See sources cited by James Charlesworth in *Bulletin of the John Rylands Library*, 60(Spring 1978):388, notes 3-6, and p. 389, notes 1-2.

63

15. David W. Hughes, "The Star of Bethlehem," *Nature*, 264(December 9, 1976):513.

16. Hoehner, *Chronological Aspects*, pp. 31-37.

17. "Isaac," *Encyclopaedia Judaica* (Jerusalem: Keter Publishing House, Ltd., 1971), pp. 3-4.

18. Ibid., "Midrash," pp. 1508-13.

19. *Midrash Rabbah—Exodus*, S.M. Lehrman, trans. (London: Soncino Press, 1939), pp. 227-28.

20. Ibid.

21. Maurice Liber, *Rashi*, translated from the French by Adele Szold (Philadelphia: Jewish Publication Society, 1906).

22. Shemaryahu Talmon, "The Calendar Reckoning of the Sect from the Judean Desert," *Scripta Hierosolymitana*, 4, C. Rabin and Y. Yadin, eds. (Jerusalem: Magnes Press, 1958), p. 183.

23. Abba Hillel Silver, *Messianic Speculation in Israel* (New York, 1927).

24. T. H. Gaster, *Dead Sea Scriptures* (New York: Doubleday & Company, Inc., 1964).

25. Ibid., p. 47.

26. Talmon, "The Calendar Reckoning of the Sect."

27. Gaster, *Dead Sea Scriptures*, p. 3. See also G. Vermes, *The Dead Sea Scrolls in English* rev. ed. (New York: Penguin, 1968), p. 13.

28. Hoehner, *Chronological Aspects*, pp. 81-90.

29. Arthur Spier, *The Comprehensive Hebrew Calendar* (New York: Behrman House Inc., 1952).

30. Matthew 26:2, 17-19; Mark 14:1, 12-16; Luke 22:1, 7-8, 13-15.

31. Richard A. Parker, *The Calendar of Ancient Egypt*, Studies in Ancient Oriental Civilization, no. 26 (Chicago: University of Chicago Press, 1950).

32. O'Neil, *Time and Calendars*, p. 63.

33. John L. Sorenson, "The Significance of an Apparent Relationship Between the Ancient Near East and Mesoamerica," in C. L. Riley, J. C. Kelley, C. W. Pennington, and R. L. Rands, eds., *Man Across the Sea: Problems of Pre-Columbian Contacts* (London/Austin: University of Texas Press, 1971), pp. 219-41.

34. "The Maya, Children of Time," *National Geographic*, vol. 148, no. 6 (December 1975), p. 729.

35. John Eric S. Thompson, *Maya Hieroglyphic Writing—An Introduction* (Norman: University of Oklahoma Press, 1971), p. 104. See also M. Wells Jakeman, *The Ancient Middle-American Calendar System: Its Origin and Development*, Publications in Archaeology and Early History, no. 1 (Provo, Utah: Brigham Young University, 1947).

36. When counting the number of years from BC. to A.D., keep in mind that the length of time from 1 B.C. to 1 A.D. is only one year. There is no "zero" year between the end of that time which we call *before Christ* and that time which we call *anno Domini* (A.D.). Thus from 2 B.C. to the middle of A.D. 2 is three years and *not* four, or from April 1 B.C. to April A.D. 33 is 33 years and not 34 years.

37. Joseph Smith, *History of the Church* 1:75-79.

38. Ibid., pp. 336-37.

Table 1 Notes

1. At the beginning of the first century there appear to have been three systems used in Judea for determining when a day began: The Romans favored the midnight-to-midnight scheme; the Sadducees used the sunset-to-sunset mode of reckoning; and the Pharisees, Essenes, and Galileans seem to have relied on a sunrise-to-sunrise style. This point has no immediate significance for the birth of Christ, but becomes important later when we attempt to harmonize the synoptic reckoning of Passover and the Last Supper with the reckoning of Passover found in the Gospel of John. For more information on the different reckonings of the day see Harold W. Hoehner, *Chronological Aspects of the Life of Christ* (Grand Rapids: Zondervan Publishing House, 1977), pp. 81-90; Julian Morgenstern, "Supplementary Studies in the Calendars of Ancient Israel," *Hebrew Union College Annual*, 10:15-38; Solomon Zeitlin, "The Beginning of the Jewish Day during the Second Commonwealth," *The Jewish Quarterly Review*, 36:403-14. For a good treatment of the functioning of the Hebrew calendar see Arthur Spier, *The Comprehensive Hebrew Calendar* (New York: Behrman House, Inc., 1952), and Edgar Frank, *Talmudic and Rabbinical Chronology: The System of Counting Years in Jewish Literature* (New York: Philip Feldheim, Inc.), 1953.

2. See footnote 1.

3. The times of the astronomical new and full moons are taken from Herman H. Goldstine, *New and Full Moons 1001 B.C. to A.D. 1651* (Philadelphia: American Philosophical Society, 1973). The times were originally calculated for an observer in Babylon (Bagdad). Using Greenwich time as a base, Jerusalem time is one hour west of Babylon.

4. Even though the astronomical new moon occurred in the early afternoon of March 19, the crescent of the new moon would not have been visible to the naked eye until the evening of March 20. See Joseph Ashbrook, "Astronomical Scrapbook: Some Very Thin Lunar Crescents," *Sky and Telescope*, August 1971, pp. 78-79.

5. Jesus was born on Nisan 14 in two schemes of reckoning, and during the night the Passover meal was celebrated among the Pharisees and Galileans.

6. Luke 2:8 suggests that the birth of our Lord occurred during the night. The midnight in the table does not mean to imply that that was the exact hour of our Lord's birth. It is nothing more than a reference point from which 1,830 solar years are measured. The reference point is used to establish the necessary degree of tolerance in determining the harmony of April 6.

7. See Numbers 38:16-25, Exodus 34:18, and Deuteronomy 16:1-8.

Table 2 Notes

1. Helaman 14:2-9.
2. Helaman 16:9.
3. 3 Nephi 1:4.
4. Goldstine, *New and Full Moons*.
5. 3 Nephi 1:11-14.

Table 4 Notes

1. Table 4 brings all the chronological calculations from this work together into one convenient reference. It shows the relationships and dates for Christ's birth, Christ's death and resurrection, and the restoration of Christ's church. It is a single source that one can use to check and recheck the fit of April 6, 1830, to other events. As such it explains the chronology. The footnotes and references should prove helpful to those who wish to inquire into the chronology of these events even more fully.

2. The birth of Christ occurred during the night in Bethlehem (Luke 2: 8-11) and during the day in America (3 Nephi 1:19). The time difference between Judea and North America varies from six to twelve hours and for South America from five to seven hours. The nine-hour difference between Jerusalem and America in the table is only a midpoint among the various time zones of North and South America.

3. Christ died on Friday, Nisan 14, in the ninth hour after sunrise, i.e. 3:00 p.m. (Matthew 27:46; Mark 15:34-37.)

4. The resurrection occurred on the morning of the first day of the week following Christ's death. (John 20:1-18.)

5. D&C 20:1.

6. In 1582 Joseph Scaliger devised the Julian Period and named it after his father Julius—not after the Julian calendar. It has since become a method used by astronomers to number and identify days from noon, January 1, 4713 B.C. to the present. See George E. Deluny (ed.), *The World Almanac and Book of Facts 1978*, New York: Newspaper Enterprise Association, Inc., 1977, p. 785. The Julian date allows one to calculate quickly and accurately the time between events. The Julian dates in the table were checked against both the Julian and Gregorian calendar dates by the U.S. Naval Observatory, Nautical Almanac Office, Washington, D.C. on December 22, 1977.

7. Calendar Systems:

Gregorian calendar. Pope Gregory XIII introduced this calendar in 1582 to correct a slight error in the Julian calendar. The Gregorian calendar has since become the most common calendar of the world today. See *World Almanac 1978*, p. 788. Christ's birth, death and resurrection are identified in the Gregorian calendar even though that calendar system was not devised until the late sixteenth century.

Julian calendar. The Julian calendar began on January 1, 45 B.C., and for the first thirty-six years the Romans intercalated once every third year instead of every fourth year. To correct the error, Emperor Augustus omitted intercalary days between 8 B.C. and A.D. 4, which meant that the Julian calendar date of April 7, 1 B.C., was for the Roman world April 6. See *Encyclopedia Britannica* (1973), "Calendar," p. 601.

Hebrew calendar. The months and days of the Hebrew calendar are determined by the cycles of the moon and the sun. All the dates in the table have been calculated on the basis of when the new lunar crescent in the spring was visible over Jerusalem. See Spier, *Hebrew Calendar*, and footnote 1, Table 1.

Nephite calendar. The specific date of Christ's death in the Nephite calendar is found in 3 Nephi 8:5. The civil calendar of ancient America was fixed with 365 days. See John Eric S. Thompson, *Maya Hieroglyphic Writing—An Introduction* (Norman: University of Oklahoma Press, 1971), p. 104. See also Broughton Richmond, *Time Measurement and Calendar Construction* (Netherlands: E. J. Brill, Leiden, 1956), pp. 98, 103, 118.

8. Astronomical Data:

Length of solar year. The solar or tropical year is slowly decreasing by about 5.3 seconds per 1,000 years. By taking this fact into consideration it is possible to improve the calculation of the length of time from 1 B.C. to A.D. 1830 by about five hours. See O'Neil, *Time and Calendars,* p. 22.

New moon and full moon. The times of the new and full moons are taken from Goldstine, *New and Full Moons* and Berenic L. Morrison, *Phases of the Moon 1800-1959,* Circular No. 112, Washington, D.C.: United States Naval Observatory, April 8, 1966. All times are expressed in Jerusalem time, which is two hours east of Greenwich time.

Index